The MAD® COOLER

#78

WARNER BOOKS

A Warner Communications Company

THE FARCE BE WITH YOU! DEPT.

A couple of years ago, they made a movie called "Star Wars." It was a smash hit, so they announced that they would make a sequel. Everybody thought it would be called "Star Wars II"... but, lo and behold, they called it "Episode V"! Which means that "Star Wars" was actually "Star Wars IV," and "Star Wars VI" through "X" will be made after "V" but before "I" through "III"! In any case, they'd better surpass this sequel, which doesn't compare to the original! In fact . . .

STAR

THE EMPIRE STRIKES OUT

BORES

ARTIST: MORT DRUCKER   WRITER: DICK DE BARTOLO

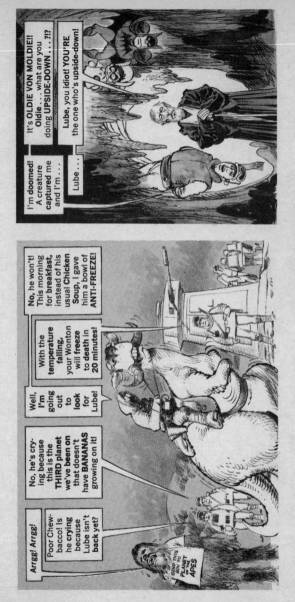

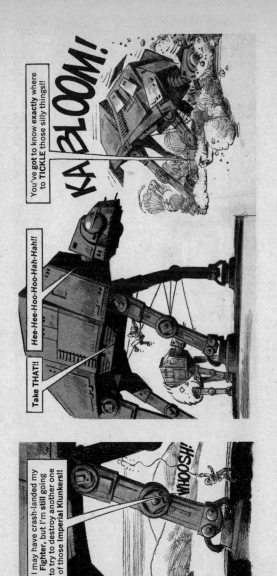

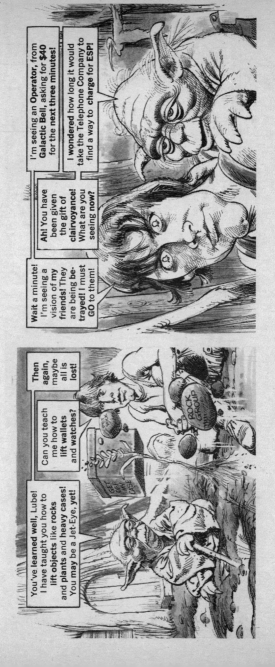

Get angry at me, Lube! When your anger starts, your power ceases!
Get ANGRY at you? Whatever for? I don't GET angry! Besides, I put on one of those extra dry deodorants this morning! I'm calm and cool and I have no underarm wetness!
Okay, Lube! You asked for it! Now let's see you get angry! I've cut off one of your hands! What do you say to that??
I APPLAUD you! Only it's not going to be TOO LOUD!
I have more gooc news! I am your Father!!
No! No! It can't be . . . !
That's it! You're getting angry! I AM your Father! What are you going to do about it!?
I'm NOT going to send you a Father's Day card, if that's what you're hinting at!!
In that case, I push you off this planet . . . and into the void of space!!
You're certainly MEAN enough to be my old man!!

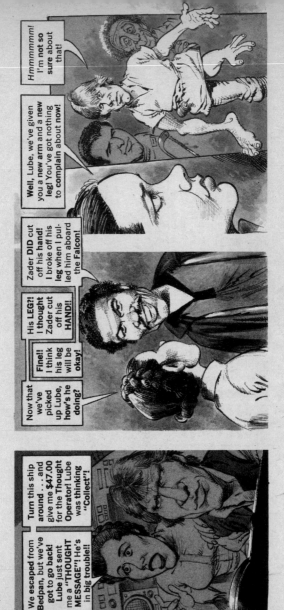

...AND SO ENDS EPISODE V OF "STAR BORES"!

★ ★ ★ ★

WHEN LANDOUGH AND CHEWBACCO FIND THE FROZEN HAM YOYO, WILL HE CONTINUE TO GIVE PRINCESS LAIDUP THE COLD SHOULDER?

★ ★ ★ ★

WILL CREEPIO KEEP BABBLING ON ENDLESSLY, AND FINALLY BE ELECTED TO PUBLIC OFFICE?

★ ★ ★ ★

WILL DART ZADER STOP BEING "MR. NICE GUY," AND REALLY TRY TO DESTROY LUBE SKYSTALKER?

★ ★ ★ ★

WILL ANY OF US REALLY CARE WHAT HAPPENS, AFTER ANOTHER TWO-YEAR INTERMISSION...??

There goes Landough and Chewbacco in the Falcon! I thought we should try to find HamYoyo, and I ordered them to set a course of N-30°—W-17°!

But, Princess...the ship with Ham and the Bounty Hunters was last seen going in the opposite direction!

I KNOW! I said we should try to find Ham Yoyo! I DIDN'T SAY we were in any particular hurry!

DON MARTIN TAKES ANOTHER LOOK AT FIREMEN

THWOCK!

MORE MAD CANDID SNAPSHOTS OF HISTORICAL CELEBRITIES

ARTIST & WRITER: PAUL PETER PORGES

YOUNG KING DAVID TRAINS FOR HIS UPCOMING BOUT

ADOLPH HITLER INVENTS THE GOOSESTEP

QUEEN VICTORIA IS SLIGHTLY AMUSED

DR. LIVINGSTON MEETS HIS FIRST TRIBE OF PYGMIES

YOUNG EMPEROR NERO'S FIRST VIOLIN TEACHER, SHORTLY BEFORE HE QUITS

WM. SHAKESPEARE SHOWS HIS CONTEMPT FOR SOME BAD FIRST-NIGHT REVIEWS

CLEOPATRA CONTEMPLATES HAVING A NOSE JOB PERFORMED

KING MIDAS OVER-TIPS AS HE LEAVES PALACE BANQUET

CHRISTOPHER COLUMBUS WITH EARLIER MODELS OF THE EARTH

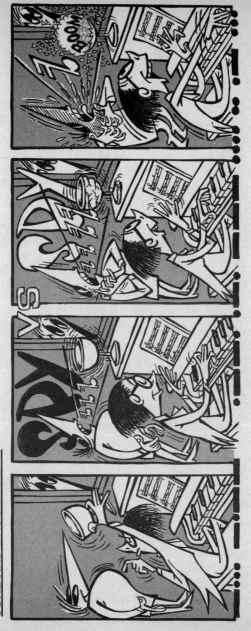

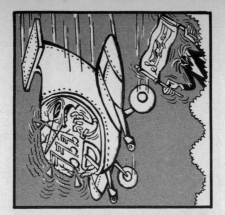

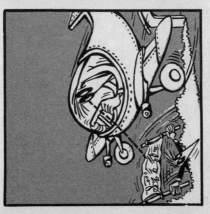

Don't you just love it when you run to your mail box in hopes of finding that somebody's sent you five bucks for some old debt because you haven't paid your rent and you don't have a dime for food . . . but the only letter there is a piece of junk mail that starts out: *"We know you are the kind of man who appreciates the value of a well-made $300 suit, which is why this offer is being sent to men like you!"* Well, we wonder what other goofs are being made because of . . .

MIXED-UP JUNK MAIL MAILING LISTS

ARTIST: HARRY NORTH, ESQ.   WRITER: DICK DE BARTOLO

Dear Potential Homeowner:

"White Oaks" is no ordinary housing development, and that's why this pre-opening offer is not going to everyone! Located almost entirely within Wasp Woods, "White Oaks" will be an exclusive residential community made up of the most desirable families. So if you're the type of person we're looking for, why not come out to "White Oaks" today, and let us show you our planned private community of Luxury

Dear Home Handyperson:

What's your next home improvement? A finished basement? A swimming pool? A guest room?

Whatever your plans, "Home Handyperson Magazine" can help you with any of these projects, and

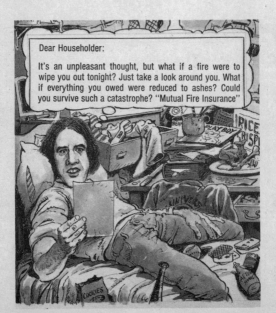

DON
LOOKS
FIRE

MARTIN
AT
MEN

GRRRRRR...

This is the introductory verse to an amusing song performed by the title character in "The Mikado." In it, Gilbert and Sullivan then proceed to list their pet hates and the punishments they'd like to see meted out. But since 'The Mikado' was written in 1885, those pet hates are now outdated. Which is why MAD feels it's time for

A "Let The Punishment Fit The Crime" Up-Date

The Nuclear Power Apologists who
call all our fears unbased:
  Their attics and basements
  Will serve as encasements
For radioactive waste!

The greedy Professional Athlete
whose salary hikes never cease:
A turnstile he's chained to
So he can explain to
Fans why admissions increase!

The Reckless Driving Highway Clod
who has to be finally checked:
    He'll learn pain and grief well
    On some cloverleaf hell
Where all the exits connect!

The Disco Freak in public places
whose giant tape-player blares:
His tapes, we will loot them
And then substitute them
With hymns and Irish folk airs!

Our project so decreed
Is all but guaranteed
        To make the penalty
            fit the deed,
The penalty
    fit the deed;
And ev'ry crime will be
An opportunity
        To try a little
            frivolity,
        A little frivolity!

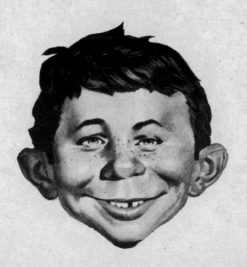

The Sidewalk Roller Skating Creep
who knocks you right off your feet:
We'll force him to travel
O'er pot holes and gravel
While cab-dodging in the street!

The rabid White Supremacist
whose tolerance really rots:
We'll gather their legions
And ship them to regions
Like Harlem and Hough and Watts!

The Over-Spending Bureaucrat
whose budget's destined to bust:
His debts, we've enacted
Will all be contracted
To "Mafia Loan & Trust"!

The preaching Religious Fanatics
who babble, chatter and stare:
They'll all be sequestered
And thoroughly pestered
By Madalyn Murray O'Hair!

The Punk Rock Band whose musical
talents obviously don't exist:
They're helped by obtaining
Remedial training
In Beethoven, Brahms and Liszt!

The sneaky Real Estate Promoters
who change swamps into gold:
We'll only let buy land
Around Three Mile Island
And sell 'til all of it's sold!

The Fiends Who Write Those TV Ads
  that have us all revolted:
      They'll all meet their doom
      In a huge screening room
(Whose doors are locked and bolted!)

        We'll make them watch an endless show
          of all they've e'er begat:
              Every (yecch!) bathtub ring;
              Stupid products that sing;
        Clod "Whipple" and "Morris The Cat"!

A MAD
LOOK AT...
TRA

AIR
VEL

ARTIST & WRITER:
SERGIO ARAGONES

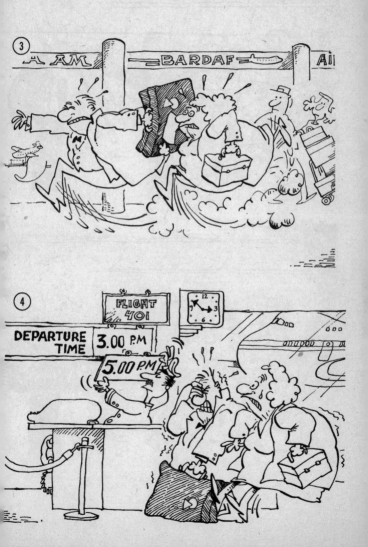

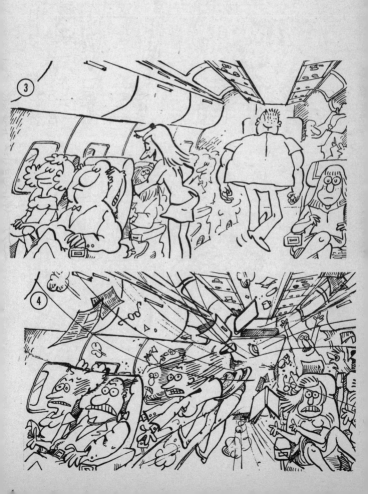

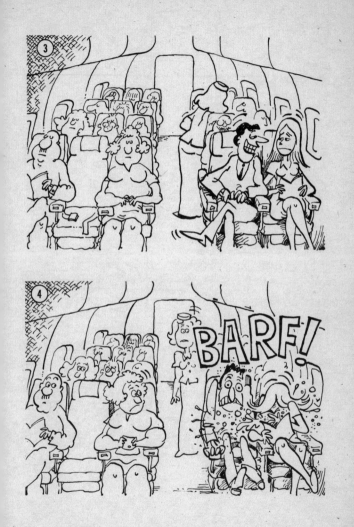

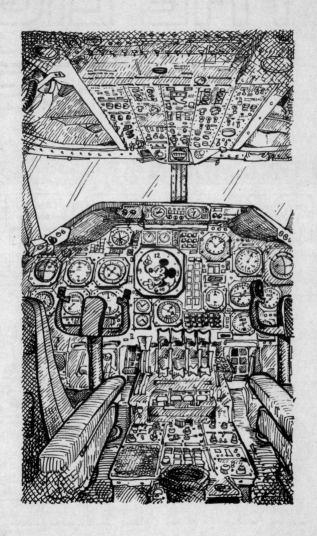

THE LIG SIDE

PUNISHMENT

HTER
OF...

ARTIST & WRITER:
DAVE BERG

SUCCESS

GADGETS

MAKING ENDS MEET

BREAKING UP

You ask why I'm **sitting** here like this? I just got a **divorce!**

But . . . you **weren't** even married! You were only living together!

The **break-up** hurts just as much as if we had a **legal document!** The **relationship** was the **same** as if we were **man and wife!** Everything we did, we **did together!** Everything was "us" . . . and "we" . . . and "ours" . . . equally!

STUDYING

Yes, I'm **watching** it! It's a **fascinating** TV show . . . !

Oh, by the way! Did you hear about **Cathy** and **Herb!** Yep! It's "splitsville" . . . !

TAP TAP

INTRUDERS

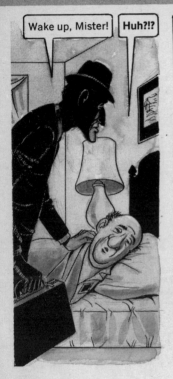

AMBITION

BULLYING

THE ECONOMY

BUREAUCRACY

ATHLETICS

ARE HAPPY

ARTIST: PAUL COKER

ARE YOU HAPPY NOW . . .

. . . that you finally got your kid to take up the violin . . . and he loves it so much, he won't stop playing it?

YOU NOW...?

WRITER: FRANK JACOBS

ARE YOU HAPPY NOW . . .

. . . that you got your boyfriend to see a shrink about his problem . . . and the solution is that he should dump you?

ARE YOU HAPPY NOW . . .

. . . that you nagged your daughter into ditching the goon she was dating . . . and she's going with an even bigger schmuck?

ARE YOU HAPPY NOW . . .

. . . that you finally got your Boss to give you a big job with "more responsibility" . . . and you can't handle it?

ARE YOU HAPPY NOW...

... that you've worked hard and finally amassed all the money you'll ever need ... and you're too old to enjoy it?

ARE YOU HAPPY NOW...

... that you succeeded in losing those 40 pounds ... and replacing your entire wardrobe is gonna cost you four grand?

ARE YOU HAPPY NOW . . .

. . . that the Superstar your team paid half a million, to win the pennant, has finally united the team—against him?

ARE YOU HAPPY NOW . . .

. . . that you finally made a small profit on that stock you held for years . . . and inflation has wiped out the gain?

ARE YOU HAPPY NOW . . .

. . . that you got your agnostic kid to "take a look at religion" . . . and he's become a fanatic in some weird cult?

ARE YOU HAPPY NOW . . .

. . . that the political party you hate has been voted out . . . and the winner you supported is doubling your taxes?

ARE YOU HAPPY NOW . . .

. . . that you've finally turned 18, and you're allowed to see those "X-Rated" movies . . . and you find them a big bore?

ARE YOU HAPPY NOW . . .

. . . that you've managed to keep all your New Year's resolutions . . . and life for you has become a total bore?

ARE YOU HAPPY NOW . . .

. . . that you persuaded your Wife to join a "Swinging Couples" group . . . and she loves it . . . and you don't?

ARE YOU HAPPY NOW . . .

. . . that you finally got the nerve to move out of your parents' house . . . and your roommate is even more of a nag?

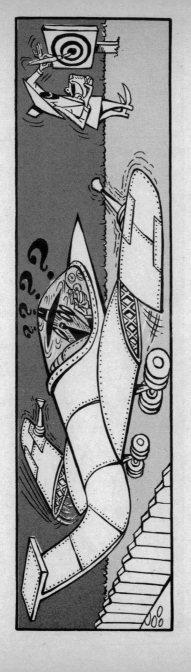

A while back (MAD #210), we presented a collection of easily memorized insults about famous people, places and things that were all designed to help even the biggest clod become an instant Don Rickles. This valuable guide to possible popularity and probable hits in the head was appropriately entitled "The MAD Nasty Book." It was tolerated without too many reader complaints presumably because we promised that it would be the only edition we'd make you endure. But, as you may be starting to suspect, that's the nasty thing about Nasty Books. They vow you won't ever have to suffer through another one, and then they make you do it anyway. So grit your teeth and brace yourself for—

THE

MAD

NASTY

BOOK

VOLUME TWO

ARTIST: HARRY NORTH, ESQ.   WRITER: TOM KOCH

THE KU KLUX KLAN

1. ...is something like a college fraternity, except that its members are all too dumb to get into college.

2. ...wears bed sheets so the guys won't give away their deepest secret: underneath, they all have on dresses.

3. ...defends Christian brotherhood by hanging anyone suspected of opposing it.

4. ...makes a lot of speeches, but, fortunately, in such a thick redneck drawl that they can't be understood.

5. ...encourages members to put pillowcases over their heads as a means of improving their appearance.

COMPUTERS

1. ... save money for corporations by passing employee errors along to the customers to figure out.

2. ... are labor saving devices that can be programmed to play chess with each other so people won't have to.

3. ... require less than a second to put a thousand pieces of mistaken information into alphabetical order.

4. ... take faulty addition that could be corrected with a pencil and put it on tape where it's preserved forever.

5. ... are so intelligent that they even set the type for printing this article this article this article.

MORK & MINDY

1. ... is comforting to watch because it portrays creatures from other planets as being too stupid to cause trouble.

2. ... is aired by A.B.C. to make "Three's Company" and "Charlie's Angels" look like intellectual programming by comparison.

3. ... provides Robin Williams with a perfect showcase for all one of his talents.

4. ... enriched our culture by adding "nanoo-nanoo" and "shazbat" to the English language.

5. ... is filled with such great actors that they're capable of covering up their embarrassment over appearing on the show.

CHER

1. . . . has a terrific shape, in the opinion of those who get turned on by looking at a pencil.

2. . . . doesn't really have a crack in her voice; she just likes to practice yodeling while she talks.

3. . . . wears revealing gowns in public because nothing else she does seems to attract much attention.

4. . . . deserves the thanks of a grateful nation for keeping Sonny Bono off welfare for all those years.

5. . . . proved ·that only in America can broken marriages and illicit affairs be parlayed into fame and fortune.

U.S. DEPT. OF ENERGY

1. . . . hopes to perfect solar power within 20 years after the last person in the country has frozen to death.

2. . . . saw the 1974 Arab oil boycott coming as long ago as 1977.

3. . . . thinks everyone should keep warm the same way its employees do—by shuffling papers.

4. . . . insists that the 55 M.P.H. speed limit conserves home heating oil by keeping Americans out on the highway longer.

5. . . . maintains the thermostats in its offices at 65 degrees—throughout July and August.

MIKE WALLACE

1. ...has built a big audience for "60 Minutes" among viewers who hope to see him get flattened.

2. ...hopes he never gets sick because he's already accused every doctor in the country of being a quack.

3. ...intimidates those he interviews so they'll be afraid to comment on his cheap hair dye job.

4. ...may be the only person in New York who is fighting mad about crooked bingo games in Wyoming.

5. ...is upset because he can't think of any more corporations to accuse of manufacturing poison fertilizer.

PETE ROSE

1. . . . holds records for hitting in 44 consecutive games and flopping in 31 consecutive TV commercials.

2. . . . drives a Rolls-Royce so parking lot attendants won't think he's just some crude lout who uses bad grammar.

3. . . . is one of the few active players capable of joining a division champ and taking it all the way to fourth place.

4. . . . has never been injured by debris thrown from the bleachers because, fortunately, it all hit him on the head.

5. . . . isn't concerned about maintaining a macho image—and he'll punch any pansy in the mouth who says he is.

THE REPUBLICAN PARTY

1. . . . brags about having produced Abraham Lincoln and Dwight Eisenhower, but hardly ever mentions Warren Harding or Richard Nixon.

2. . . . has a program to solve all the problems of 1926, in case that year ever comes back.

3. . . . claims that every one of its hair brained schemes is designed to whip Communism.

4. . . . is totally without leadership, now that John Wayne is gone.

5. . . . doesn't really hate the poor; it only hates the poor who organize labor unions.

THE DEMOCRATIC PARTY

1. . . . brags about having produced John Kennedy and Franklin Roosevelt, but hardly ever mentions Lyndon Johnson or Grover Cleveland.

2. . . . has 238 programs to benefit those who are willing to vote, but unwilling to work.

3. . . . claims that every one of its hair brained schemes is designed to whip big business.

4. . . . is totally without leadership, now that Shirley MacLaine has gone back to Hollywood.

5. . . . doesn't really hate the rich; it only hates the rich who somehow avoid the 70% tax bracket.

THE AIRLINE INDUSTRY

1. . . . has no flights into Muncie, Indiana, because that's the airport it uses to hide your lost luggage.

2. . . . thoughtfully provides every passenger with a gourmet meal and a barf bag to throw it up into.

3. . . . can fly you from the Chicago Airport to New York in less time than it takes to drive from Chicago to the Chicago Airport.

4. . . . offers first class service to those who are willing to pay 53 dollars extra for a free martini.

5. . . . makes certain that its two flights a day between the same cities are always scheduled at 7:15 A.M. and 7:30 A.M

JANE FONDA

1. . . . is capable of debating world affairs with some of the deepest thinkers in Hollywood.

2. . . . looks a little like Mary Tyler Moore, and sounds a lot like your strange uncle who lives in a tree.

3. . . . vows to get her husband into public office, even if she has to buy him his own country.

4. . . . tries to prove that she's not like her father, who had nothing going for him except talent and common sense.

5. . . . joins other celebrities who have become molders of public opinion, such as Jerry Lewis and Smoky the Bear.

TV COMMERCIALS

1. . . . have a knack for making a 30-second message seem longer than a half-hour program.

2. . . . teach us that we can all achieve success and happiness, once we stop smelling bad.

3. . . . conduct comparison tests between competing products so we can decide for ourselves that we don't care which one wins.

4. . . . make us wonder how doctors survive when all the medical advice we need is available from neighborhood druggists.

5. . . . never explain how the $4,999 cars they describe always cost $8,000 when we go to buy one.

THE CHRYSLER CORP.

1. ... needs to sell its remaining 1980 cars so it'll have room for the 1979s that are being recalled for defects.

2. ... shows great aptitude for going into some other line of production, such as raising turkeys.

3. ... is finally getting what it deserves for making all those 1957 De-Sotos with huge tail fins.

4. ... will start research on an economy car if we'll put up the cash by buying its left-over gas guzzlers.

5. ... had to ask the government for money because no private organizations specialize in rewarding incompetence.

DOLLY PARTON

1. . . . is five-feet-four-inches tall, if you count the eighteen inches of hair piled on top.

2. . . . is so talented that she's famous for two separate things: the right one and the left one.

3. . . . got rid of her rural accent by studying at the Billy Carter School of Speech.

4. . . . spent $100,000 converting a bus into a motor home because people who sing like her have to keep moving.

5. . . . took a bust development course so no one would notice that the rest of her is fat, too.

PEOPLE MAGAZINE

1. . . . is a great publication for those who never learned how to read hard things, such as two syllable words.

2. . . . leads its regular subscribers to assume that Eric Estrada is the most important person in the country today.

3. . . . differs from the National Enquirer chiefly in the fact that it's printed on slick paper.

4. . . . has succeeded because a whole issue can be read during a one-minute TV commercial.

5. . . . provides scholarly research material for anyone writing a thesis on "The Sex Life Of Rock Musicians."

ONE DAY IN THE LIFE OF SOME SALESMEN

A COLLECTION OF **MAD**

X-RAYVINGS

ARTIST: BOB CLARKE   WRITER: DON EDWING

PUT YOUR FUNNY WHERE YOUR MOUTH IS! DEPT.

AN AL JAFFEE

SNAPPY ANSWERS TO STUPID QUESTIONS

Gangland Episode

One of the most popular books in recent years is "The Book Of Lists." It's loaded with lists, such as "11 Prominent Coffee Drinkers," "10 Famous Snorers," "17 Animals With Pouches" and "The 12 Heaviest Humans." The only problem is: the book doesn't have much to do with everyday living! So MAD has done its usual thing, and now presents—

MAD'S REALLY RELEVANT BOOK OF LISTS

WRITER: FRANK JACOBS

THE 8 EXPRESSIONS CAUSING THE GREATEST FEAR

1. "It's spreading."
2. "The I.R.S. is calling."
3. "Hold it right there, muthuh."
4. "I *am* trying to stop!"
5. "We're not alone."
6. "You're being traded to Cleveland."
7. "I can't kill it."
8. "There's no cause for alarm."

THE 8 MOST EFFECTIVE MEDICAL COP-OUTS

1. "It's going around."
2. "It's all in your mind."
3. "It's probably inherited."
4. "It's too early to tell."
5. "It's too late to do anything."
6. "We'll run some tests."
7. "We'll run more tests."
8. "The tests are inconclusive."

9 VERY UNSUCCESSFUL PICK-UP LINES

1. "Would you like to see my boa constrictor?"
2. "Is that a false nose?"
3. "You look just like a hooker I knew in Fresno."
4. "I'm drunk."
5. "Hi, my friends call me Creepy."
6. "Would you like to come to a party in my toolshed?"
7. "I just threw up."
8. "You're ugly but you intrigue me."
9. "I had to find out what kind of woman would go out dressed like that."

9 LEAST INSPIRED MAD PREMISES

1. The Lighter Side of Terrorism
2. Terminal Diseases to Match Your Career
3. You Know You Should Change Your Sex When . . .
4. Hysterical Logarithms
5. Don Martin Looks At Tulsa
6. If Famous Celebrities Were Into Strip-Mining
7. The Degenerate's Mother Goose
8. Mad's Busboy of the Year
9. If Albanian Women Played Baseball

6 SUREFIRE LINES TO GET HIM TO BREAK OFF THE RELATIONSHIP

1. "I do karate chops in my sleep."
2. "I'm into not bathing."
3. "I collect dead spiders and keep them in jars in my closet."
4. "I start out the day with raw onions."
5. "I'm pregnant and I don't know who the father is."
6. "My Uncle Vito and his capo want to talk to you."

9 PIECES OF FLATTERY WE COULD DO WITHOUT

1. "You're a helluva good loser."
2. "You're really terrific to put up with my playing around."
3. "You're lucky—most men would have fractured *both* arms."
4. "You're brave—most men would have passed out from the pain."
5. "You take insults beautifully."
6. "You may not be good-looking, but you're sweet."
7. "You've been calm and cool all through this earthquake."
8. "You've taken your bankruptcy like a man."
9. "You never flinched when they mugged us."

6 COMMENTS TO AVOID MAKING WITH A WOMEN'S LIBBER

1. "What's happening, baby?"
2. "Whaddya expect from a woman driver?"
3. "You're an elegant broad."
4. "She does it as well as a guy."
5. "What do you think of girl jocks?"
6. "So long, kid."

8 MEMORABLE MODERN DISASTERS

1. The Susan B. Anthony dollar
2. Billy Carter
3. "Star Trek—the Motion Picture"
4. The San Diego Padres
5. Ilie Nastase
6. "The Gong Show"
7. The U.S. Postal Service
8. "Super Train"

7 POLITE COMMENTS YOU CAN MAKE TO A BORE WHICH SOUND LIKE YOU'RE LISTENING WHEN YOU'RE REALLY NOT

1. "Is that so?"
2. "Go on."
3. "Interesting."
4. "I didn't know that."
5. "Mmmm."
6. "Mmmm?"
7. "Mmmm!"

8 NAMES NOT TO NAME YOUR BABY BOY

1. Attila
2. Rasputin
3. Darth
4. Rover
5. Richard Milhous
6. Ayatollah
7. Satan
8. Betty Sue

THE 7 LEAST BELIEVABLE COMMENTS

1. "Your check is in the mail."
2. "This won't hurt."
3. "I don't do this with every guy."
4. "He won't bite."
5. "I've got the perfect girl for you."
6. "No jury would ever convict you."
7. "Give us a call the next time you're in town."

8 TOPICS TO STEER CLEAR OF AT A FORMAL DINNER

1. Descriptions of bread-mold.
2. Coping with the runs in Mexico.
3. Slaughter methods at the Chicago Stockyards.
4. Trunk murderers.
5. Raw sewage.
6. Leprosy.
7. Torture techniques in Turkish prisons.
8. Jungle rot.

THE 8 LEAST COMFORTING
PIECES OF GOOD NEWS

1. "Be glad it's only your transmission."
2. "We only have to pull the front ones."
3. "We know who fire-bombed your house."
4. "At least they didn't steal the silver."
5. "With good behavior, you'll be out in 10 years."
6. "He's alive—what's left of him."
7. "The blotches will disappear in time."
8. "Don't kill him—just work him over."

7 UNSOLVED MYSTERIES
OF MODERN MAN

1. Why is the shirt you want to buy available in every size but yours?
2. Why does your air-conditioner conk out during the worst heat-wave of the year?
3. Why does that celebrated "cold pill" bring relief to everyone but you?
4. Why does your plane leave from the most distant gate in the terminal?
5. No matter how many peanuts there are in a bowl, why do you eat all of them?
6. In a bar, why does the most obnoxious drunk strike up a conversation with you?
7. Why isn't this article listed in "The 9 Least Inspired Mad Premises?"

ONE DAY IN THE LIFE OF A TENNIS PRO

There have been TV shows about some pretty dull professions: School Teachers, Bar Tenders, Auto Mechanics, Brewery Workers, Junk Dealers, etc. Mostly, these shows were just boring, and put you to sleep! But there's one long-running series about a real far-out profession: a Medical Examiner (which is fancy for Coroner!). This program has a different effect on us. Mainly, every time we watch it, we feel . . .

Queezy

ARTIST: ANGELO TORRES   WRITER: LOU SILVERSTONE

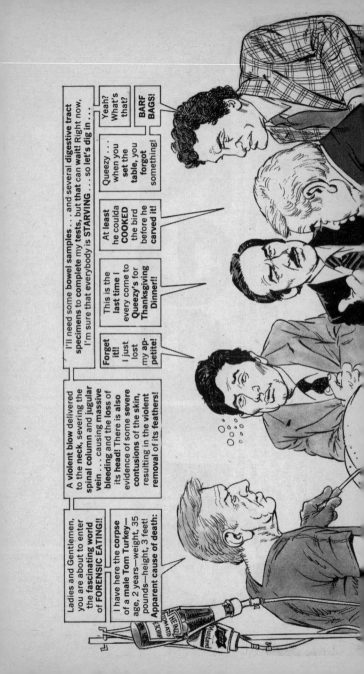

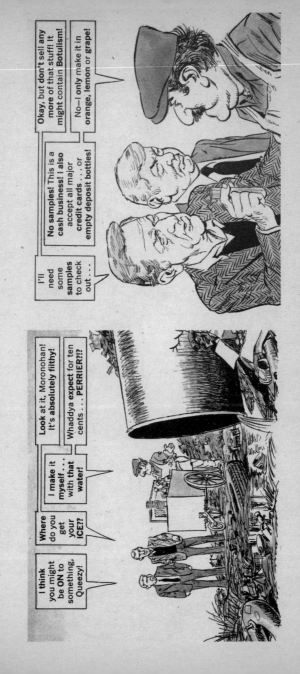

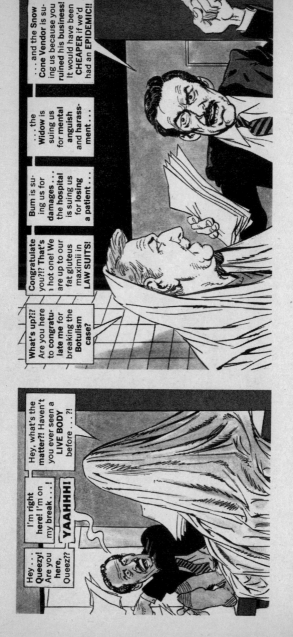